ERNA

by

Ernst Meinhard Kabaker

authorHOUSE®

AuthorHouse™
1663 Liberty Drive, Suite 200
Bloomington, IN 47403
www.authorhouse.com
Phone: 1-800-839-8640

This book is a work of non-fiction. Unless otherwise noted, the
author and the publisher make no explicit guarantees as to the
accuracy of the information contained in this book and in some

First published by AuthorHouse 2/14/2008

ISBN: 978-1-4343-5106-7 (sc)

Printed in the United States of America
Bloomington, Indiana

This book is printed on acid-free paper.

To our Mother:

We cherish your memory
We think of your life
To give it great validity
To your constant strive
To keep us all alive
We thank you into eternity!

E R N A
By Ernst Meinhard Kabaker

When there is war and ultimate great danger to life and possession the actions of the people involved become desperate and not always logical. World War II culminated in the battle around Berlin. Desperate actions by SS troops trying to defend the city unnecessarily prolonged a war, which had been decided long before then. Senseless fighting created senseless deaths, injuries and destruction.

It was April 25th, 1945. They heard some bombs explode in the distance. Ever so often the sky flamed up from the explosions. The fighting had come distinctly closer. They were both standing on the second floor of the building in which they were able to find refuge after being bombed out a few blocks away.

Hans and Erna held hands and looked at each other. "Why did we stay here? We had that safe haven out in the country." They prayed: "Lord be with us in this phase of this war!"

The Russian army had encircled Berlin and was now about to conquer it. The distant battle noise was the back ground sound for everything that went on. Warning sirens went off intermittently driving everybody into the air raid shelters. Hans poured cognac into large glasses as Erna was playing her favorite Chopin on the grand piano.

"Let us drink to a quick end to this terrible war." He pushed a glass toward Erna. The last days had given them little sleep and the constant danger of bomb explosions around them, which made them expect the worst at all times. The screams of people in the street, who were hit by pieces of bombs were singing in their ears.

"Why did you think that the Americans would be here before the Russians?" Erna said to Hans.

"Who could predict the events of this war, except that Germany is defeated?" Hans answered.

"Prost," said Erna raising her glass, let's drink to it." She continued, "We got into a terrible fix, the SS parked their ammunition and gas trucks right in front of our apartment building. They get hit, explode, and our house will go with it. I will talk with the SS soldiers about moving their trucks away from our building."

They were both descending the rear stairs, which took them to the courtyard behind the house.

"Don't do it Hans retorted, " they will have no understanding for what we fear at this time."

"I will try it anyway," Erna said. Just then a siren warned of a low flying aircraft attack.

"Go with the children into the air raid shelter," Erna told Hans. She followed the soldiers to take cover in the house across the yard.

It must have been like a volcano erupted, and the people sat on top of it, when the bomb exploded in the very building where Erna and the soldiers took refuge. There was no escape, when you were in the center of the detonation. Erna was thrown to the side and she felt a terrible pain at her left foot and right leg. There was blood all around her. The shock was too much and she lost consciousness.

When she came round she saw a nun bent over her speaking a prayer apparently in the gangway of a hospital.

"Where am I? She whispered as she felt pain shooting through her body.

"You are at the St. Gertrauden Hospital," sister Bernadette said." We'll care and pray for you". All of a sudden Erna felt herself gliding away from the pain and horror of the present and reliving some of the years past.

It was a snowy day in 1906. All the pine trees around the little house on a hill were covered with a white blanket. From the top of the hill you could see the little town of Bleicherode with its two Churches and one small synagogue.

Erna and her six year old brother Max were pulling their toboggan up the hill, and then they were sliding down together. They went up and down again and again all afternoon until it became almost dark. Then they hurried home. Their mother was standing at the door anxious to see them come in to take off their wet clothing. The warmest place in the house was the large kitchen with cooking stove. They all sat down at the table in the middle of the room, and when mother was filling their plates with her homemade chicken noodle soup Father Goldberg joined them. He also came out of the cold.

"This great soup of yours can revive anybody, Bertha." Said Carl.

Erna's face was beaming seeing her father: "Did you help a lot of sick people, father?"

"Mr. Schlesinger came to have his arm patched up, a tree fell on it and I bandaged the abrasions!" How did this happen?" Bertha asked.

"Oh, he cut down a tree for firewood, it grew too close to the house. He was lucky not to be injured worse."

"Did he thank God?" Erna asked. "You are right, he should have", was her father's response. "We never thank God enough for His kindness." After dinner Bertha lit the candles and Carl read from the Books of Moses about Israel's escape from slavery in Egypt. Today was Friday and at sundown the beginning of the Jewish Sabbath. Carl said: "If you separate the conception of morals from faith in God, you would also destroy the morals." These words were too high reaching for Erna, but her mother understood. When her mother put her hands over her head to say a Hebrew blessing, it made her feel very good.

March 1907 Erna's youngest brother, Siegfried was born. A little baby in the family was cause for a lot of excitement. The little baby required much attention. Erna loved to cuddle and take care of him, even if it meant to change his dirty diapers, which was a great help for her mother. Siggi, as they called him, quickly developed to be aware of his surroundings, and his blue eyes were firmly fixed on his sister when she combed the few brown hairs on his head. She would hold him and tenderly kiss his soft cheeks. She would pack him in the baby carriage, and take him for a walk in the nearby Park.

It was like the weeks and months flew by as the Goldberg family was actively living in the little Harz mountain town. Erna had become quite proficient on the piano and gave her first recital at the age of ten. She plaid some sonatas by Clementi and "for Elise"

by Schubert. The recital was successful and father and mother were very proud of their young daughter. Father said, "Erna, you have a promising talent, just keep it up!"

PADERBORN

Erna was twelve years old when her family moved to Paderborn, a town much larger then Bleicherode. Unlike Bleicherode it was not built in a valley surrounded by hills, but on an extended plateau leading to beautiful wooded and garden like excursion spots with fishponds etc. There are a lot of old buildings like the "Rathaus" reminding people of the town's history going back to the Middle Ages. Park like avenues surrounded the inner town with wide walking paths lined by beautiful old trees. It had a predominantly Roman Catholic population. The many beautiful churches full of colorful ornamentation gave a powerful awareness of the religious orientation of this town, the seat of a Roman Catholic bishop.

Erna entered the parochial, boys' high school which was run by the monks from the monastery in town. She and her friend Hertha were the only female exceptions in this school. She would also come home with many questions: "What does it mean to be Catholic, Father?" "They pray to Jesus and to his mother, Maria." Father Goldberg continued, "there was once a religious man, named Jesus Christ. He was a Jew like you and me, but he had exceptional gifts. People believed that he was the expected Messiah." The many things, which were new to her in this town compared to where they had lived before left Erna with many unanswered questions. Her father loved his young daughter, and he felt that it was good to keep her inquisitive mind working.

Her father had one of those new gasoline powered wagons. It had brought them from the Harz country, but he now considered trading it for a bicycle. He no longer faced the challenges of visiting his patients in out of the way places. All their furniture and belongings were transported to Paderborn on a motor driven truck, and the movers carried everything into their apartment on the Bahnhofstrasse. This apartment was much larger than the little house they lived in Bleicherode. The furniture only partially filled the rooms. There were total of three bedrooms, a bathroom with a sink and a bathtub next to the large master bedroom. Then there was a small lady's sitting room followed by a large dining room with a French connecting door to a large sitting, and music room. All these rooms were in a row opening to a long corridor, which ended at a living room for every day use. Coming back on the other side of the corridor across from the other rooms was the enormous kitchen with the wood and coal heated iron stove.

It was springtime and all the trees showed new green budding with blooms. Erna also loved to promenade with her brother, Max, down the wide walks with huge Chestnut trees on both sides. These were probably reminders of the walls surrounding this old town in the Middle Ages. Also there were the old cobblestone pavements and the old houses, put together with walls made of solid wooden (4 x 4) beams, and filled in with clay. The Town Hall (Rathaus) in particular was witness of a past, which probably went back 500 years in history. Erna was fascinated by the figurines in the elaborate water fountain in the market place in front of the "Rathaus". Erna loved to discuss her observations with her father. The town was full of people in the middle of a weekday, busy walking in various directions. "Why are they not working"? "Or are they doing something, which requires calling on their customers in homes and offices?" "You had the answer right there," said father. They took long walks in the surrounding forest and fields and father explained about the many plants, and wheat, rye and oats growing in the fields. Everything started growing, and he showed them in late summer how everything had ripened and was ready for harvesting. It was always great to come home to mother's chicken soup with noodles, and dumplings, and her spaetzle, which she served with some very good tasting meat and gravy.

After school on Tuesdays Erna and Max would walk to the house of their piano teacher. She had accomplished playing quite well, and Max was a beginner. Maybe seeing his sister playing so well, encouraged him to learn quickly. Erna took her younger brother under her wings. One day on their way home from piano lessons a group of three bigger boys attacked Max, who was walking ahead of her. Erna became annoyed, she grabbed one of the boys, she pushed him away, and she made it clear to the other two that she would not let anything happen to her brother. They dispelled quickly.

There was an electric doorbell at ground level of the house on the outside.

On the first floor, one set of stairs up the apartment was to the right and to the left were Dr. Goldberg's offices, waiting, examination, research laboratory, rooms and so on. At a medical emergency people would ring the doorbell and often Mrs. Goldberg would go downstairs to respond. As a general practitioner in this medium seize town his job never ended.

Those were relatively peaceful years in Paderborn as Erna developed from a young girl to a young lady. She completed her education at the Gymnasium in April of 1914. In May Mother and Erna traveled to Cologne to register Erna for studies at the Conservatory. The course would start in the fall! The school was impressed with Erna musical abilities.

WORLD WAR I

Germany had rapidly developed into an industrial nation and with that there were labor unions and political parties representing the various interest groups in the German Reichstag. With Mr. Bethmann Hollweg as Chancellor (Kanzler) the Kaiser Wilhelm II ran the country, thinking that he knew best contrary to his grandfather Wilhelm I, who had a skilful politician, Otto von Bismarck run the nation for him successfully. When on June 28 1914 the Austrian Archduke Franz Ferdinand was assassinated by a young Bosnian in

Sarajevo the Kaiser appeared anxious to start a war, which very quickly changed life in Germany and Europe.

The town's people were milling through the streets. There were the ones quietly going about their business. So many more were showing excitement about the occurrences of the day. The military had opened their headquarters near the town hall. Throngs of young men standing in long lines, wanting to become soldiers. Large groups of older men waving banners, expressing opposition to the Kaiser's call to arms and war! The Social Democrats were warning about war and the effects of armed conflicts. It would be hard on the bread winners of the families! The "Zentrum" party preached a message of peace and non involvement.

The students were marching in the streets to show their courage and their willingness to fight. The German National and the German "Folks" parties published their support for the Government. Older men were drinking beer in the beer halls and the "Ratskeller". At their "Stammtisch" they exchanged their experiences about the last war in 1871 as they fought in the Franco-Prussian war and the great Germany, which emerged as the result of winning this war! War conflicts would be strengthening the German fatherland, but of course victory was of the essence. Then the children were fighting war games. They were too small to understand the terrible reality of it! What thoughts get into the minds of various people, when they become aware of the threat or the cruelty of war? What people will be more affected than others? Is anybody going to profit from this? Is just the pride of a Kaiser and his people enough justification? Can we ever understand why people and especially their leaders are drawn to war?

World War I started in July of 1914. As the war progressed and wounded soldiers arrived in the Paderborn military hospital Dr. Goldberg was drafted to work at the hospital, which left him little time to take care of his regular patients. Erna volunteered at the hospital, and she received training how to take care of the soldiers, who came back with serious injuries, and who lost an arm or a leg. Every morning she walked down the main street past the railroad station, which would be an extension of the Bahnhofstrasse, where her family lived and her father had his practice as a general physician. There were always movements of soldiers at the railroad station. They were put on the trains to be transported to the front lines and equally wounded soldiers would come back to be taken to the military hospital. Erna's duty started at 8 a.m. She was assigned three beds, and she learned how to change bandages. Some of the men could not leave their beds, and they needed other assistance. As her slim and well shaped body was striding towards the hospital this morning, taking long steps, she looked like a person knowing well what she was doing and where she was going. Her pretty appearance was an enjoyment for the beholder to watch. Especially young men and soldiers could not help but have their eyes fixed on her a little longer than usual. She almost collided with an army orderly at the front door of the hospital. He smiled at her and they both continued on their way. She quickly ran up to her assigned hospital room. Many eyes followed her as she went from bed to bed to attend to her patients. "Nurse, please, help me to sit up." Or "Can you feed me, my arms cannot do it yet?" Another full day as a nurse had begun. She met the same orderly again at the front door. This time they smiled at each other in recognition that they briefly met before but Erna thought he looked debonair and handsome even though he was obviously quite a bit older than her. She was on her way home but low and behold this man followed her and caught up with her: "Excuse me," he said, "please, forgive me to be so forward! My name is Hilmar Kabaker, I felt that I have to meet you!"

Erna stopped to respond:" I am Erna Goldberg and I am in a hurry to get home." "May I talk to you to-morrow?" said the man.

"I'd like that," responded Erna.

Hilmar was of medium build with short dark hair a nice open face with a short mustache. He was certainly taller and much older than she. So the next day they shook hands, and during lunch break they walked in the courtyard of the hospital. Hilmar was obviously smitten by Erna's appearance. He could not take his eyes off her. He slowly and somewhat hesitantly explained that he had volunteered for the hospital service, and he was glad that it was only 40 kilometers from his hometown Lemgo, where his father had a cigar factory. He also had learned the trade of cigar making. Erna responded telling him that she had volunteered also as a nurse's aid, and that she was comfortable with this work since her father was a doctor and a good one, as she proudly put it. Hilmar insisted of seeing Erna again and they made a date for the following evening.

Erna was excited when she returned home that evening and when her father questioned her, because he noticed a change in her, she blushed helplessly. Erna would never forget this day. The following evening Erna and Hilmar promenaded along the park like walkways. They were looking at each other, and at first shyly he held her hand. She looked at his slim statue, he looked very masculine with his mustache, she thought. Erna showed a beautiful face line from forehead over the straight nose to the energetic chin he could see her appealing features. They were both filled with love for each other. Hilmar walked her to her parent's house and they sealed the evening with a long kiss.

From then on Hilmar and Erna saw each other every day. Hilmar would tell her about his early years in his hometown, where his father had established himself so well. Erna talked about her many ambitions and dreams which filled her young mind. Erna introduced Hilmar to her parents and mother Goldberg promptly asked him to stay for dinner that evening. Her parents liked Hilmar, and of-course it was of utmost importance to them that Hilmar was Jewish. Mother's comment was as follows: He is a nice Jewish man, but isn't he a little old for you, dear child?

The Duerkopp limousine was laboring up the steep hill in one of the Teutoburger Wald mountains. Herr Groene, the chauffeur shifted down into first gear just before reaching the top of the hill. He pushed up the rim of his cap and wiped the sweat off his forehead. Then he cautiously continued the decline in first gear, second and then in third gear. This was Erna's first ride in a limousine with Hilmar sitting next to her. They were on their way to visit with Hilmar's parents in Lemgo. They were both very excited. The first time Erna would meet Hilmar's parents. As she looked out the window she saw the thickly growing trees in the Teutoburger Wald, evergreens and then birch and maple trees intermingling.

Hilmar turned to Erna explaining that his parents were still following the old Jewish food laws. "What exactly does that mean?" asked Erna. "Well, the meat has to be kosher and the meat cannot be eaten together with any dairy products.

As they were travelling the landscape changed from a mountainous forest to a winding road lined by fruit trees going through fertile farm land. Erna was elated and she was hanging onto Hilmar excited to meet his parents and family. They finally approached Lemgo after passing through Detmold, and some small farm communities. They crossed railroad tracks, and then entered the ancient town on a bridge over the river Bega passing a water driven mill on the left and remains of the wall on both sides. The cobblestone pavement was common in a lot of old German towns. Further down Erna was impressed by the colorful well maintained very old buildings as they continued through the streets.

In the middle of town they arrived at the Kabaker's family home in the Schuhstrasse close to the cigar factory. Moritz Kabaker was standing in front of his house, and hearing the limousine approach Sara, his wife joined him. "You are welcome to our home," said Moritz, and Sara echoed: " We are so happy to meet you". Erna was overwhelmed. They embraced her heartily and welcomed her into their house. Also present were Hugo, Hilmar's older brother, and Cora, his younger sister. They all hugged Erna and welcomed her. There was a hearty meal waiting for them, which Sara had prepared. Sara kept a kosher household, and everything was prepared according to the Laws of Moses. As they sat down in the small but cozy dining room Moritz asked all for silence, and he spoke a short Hebrew blessing.

Medium sized and a strong physical appearance with his chin protruding and his straight nose rounding off at his nostrils Carl Goldberg appeared as a very resolute person. His face expressed determination to bring anything he started to a successful finish. His patients appreciated his straightforward and open manner, and they accepted his medical diagnosis with confidence. When Erna returned from her trip to Lemgo, and shared her enthusiasm about the Kabaker family he had a lot of questions. He gave all matters a deeper prospective. If there was great enthusiasm he did not want to let it wane to nothing. The momentum should be maintained, in his opinion, but he could not resist investigating as much as possible, and get a picture, which would enable him to soften the excitement to a normal attitude.

"How does Hilmar relate to your interest in music?" Oh, he enjoys music, I know!" Did you discuss some of the books, you read recently?" Erna could not remember. They talked about their lives together in the future. Hilmar described his trips to Berlin and other big cities, how he was riding a horse in the Tiergarten and did not watch for a tree branch swiping his left eye, which caused him to use glasses for better vision.

The Wedding

The hall was brightly lit, and all the guests were cheering the bride and the groom. Even though there was a war going on Hilmar and Erna were dancing, and everybody thought that they looked great together. Max (14 years old); was watching with his seven year old brother, Siggi. The adults were grouping around the rabbi, who had just married the couple. Carl Goldberg and Moritz Kabaker had a conversation about the future of their children. However everybody was sad that Sara Hilmar's mother was ill and could not be there. (She passed away a month later.) The newly weds escaped in the evening to stay at a local hotel, and took a train in the morning to Bad Pyrmont, where they spent their honeymoon.

The couple settled in a cozy little apartment not far from the army hospital where both were working. Erna had some time to get used to her life as a young housewife. The apartment had a little balcony from where she could see the street and some open fields. The farmers were hauling their produce, many other products like chickens and eggs on their horse drawn wagons to the market in town. Hilmar was on duty at the hospital, and she had a day off. Life seemed to have a new meaning for her, being pregnant, and having a concerned and caring husband. It felt good to be important to him. Her father, who in the beginning voiced his objections to her marrying so young, eventually gave her his full support, and understanding. He encouraged her to let him check on her progress in her pregnancy as her physician.

As Erna was in the middle of cleaning she heard all of a sudden an enormously loud rushing wind noise, and then an ear- splitting explosion, her house seemed to be shaken. Momentarily

Erna was so scared and confused, she threw herself on the floor thinking something was happening to her house.

Then looking out of the window she discovered a house across the street in flames with the tail end of a small airplane sticking up. Somewhat shaken she rose to see that everything was intact around her. She saw people helplessly running into the street, and in the distance she heard the ringing bell of an approaching fire engine. When her husband came home she found out more details. A German military flying student lost control of the flying machine and crashed.

The war intensified, and more people, especially young men joined the army. In 1916 Carl Goldberg was called into active duty at first in the nearby army hospital. In 1917 he was at the front line patching up the wounded in a field hospital. Also in 1917 young Max volunteered to join the army. After two months training he was shipped to the front lines in France. Late 1917 the news came to the Goldberg family that he was missing in action. Erna and her mother were devastated, and the joy was great when finally word came through the Red Cross that he was alive and a prisoner of war held by the British in France.

On April 18th 1916 Magdalena was born. She was a bundle of joy for her father and mother. Grandpa

Goldberg was delighted holding his granddaughter in his arms. "Magda (later on called Mady) is such a beautiful child, dear Erna!" he exclaimed. "She reminds me of you, when you were a baby!" He was walking with her in his arms when she slowly closed her eyes and fell asleep. "Great," said grandfather Moritz, when he was rocking Magda on his knees. "I love you my sweet little girl, and I hope that you will have a great life." When he bent over the tip of his beard tickled, and Mady smiled.

In late 1917 Hilmar's father became very ill. A virus had taken hold of his body and weakened it. He caught it from his friends. They died and so did he. There was no antidote to take the infection away. He followed his wife Sara, who passed on two years before him, into eternity.

THE TIME AFTER
WORLD WAR I

Germany lost world war one. The German Kaiser resigned in 1918. In the Versailles Treaty in 1919 the German borders were redrawn, a huge burden was imposed on the country with reparation payments, and the Rhineland was occupied by Allied troops. The new Weimar Constitution could not guarantee a stable Government, and the German Mark became heavily inflated.

Move to Lemgo

What was it like to move from a rather old town like Paderborn to a very old but much smaller town. In a smaller town everybody makes it their business to know about everybody, but especially when you are the young wife of one of the better known citizens.

Lemgo at that time with a population of about 8500 people was a small town with old houses dating back to its founding in 1190. The remains of a protecting wall remind people of a time in history when there were small invading forces trying to attack and plunder. The original wall areas had been converted into elevated wide walkways with large trees on both sides, a wonderful opportunity for walks around the whole town, for meditating or having lively conversations. Once they had settled in the town Hilmar introduced his wife to the town's prominent citizens. There was Bayer the architect, Keiser the animal doctor, Mueller the mayor, Weisbrod the principal of the boys' high school (Gymnasium), Nolting the Physician, and Pastor Eilers of the Marien Kirche.

Pastor Eilers opened the iron gate walked past a lawn area, and a few rhododendron bushes, and up the four steps leading to the front door of the house. He then pushed the doorbell button to the right. After a few minutes a young maid in a black uniform with white trim; opened the door and let him enter into the vestibule, where she politely asked him to wait a moment so she could ask the lady of the house to see him. He was then invited to enter the first room to the left. It appeared to be the music room with a giant grand piano near the windows facing the street. Minutes later the lady of the house came in and greeted him with a smile and a warm handshake. He was stunned by the great beauty of this woman sitting smiling across the table from him. His thoughts were captivated by the plush and luxurious surroundings in this room: "God has certainly blessed you richly!" he said, and then he continued: "I saw you in my church on Sunday." "Yes, that is true", said Erna. "I wanted to know more about the Christian religion. Did you say in your sermon that God loved us so much that He sent His own Son to die for our sins?" "Yes, I did, and you enter into God's grace when you accept His Son as your Savior from all the evil in the world!" Erna was very quiet for a few minutes, and then she responded: "I have to let this sink in for a while, and I may ask you more questions in the future. Thank you for your visit, *Herr Pastor*. May I offer you some fresh coffee and maybe some other refreshments?" The Pastor gratefully accepted. Looking at his hostess he asked: "How do you like Lemgo so far?" "Oh, it is a very interesting little town, and everybody has been so nice!" said Erna. "Your family has been a good influence here, beginning with your late father in law, God bless his soul." The Pastor replied

The maid knocked on the door, "Mrs. Kabaker, Mady is asking for you.' The five year old came running into the room to her mother. Erna asked to bring some cookies and Coffee. The minister and she had a long conversation about life in this small but old town.

Hilmar came home late afternoon, and Erna told him about the minister's visit. She suggested that they both visit the church again, because she liked the Pastor. Then the gardener knocked on the door to ask for instructions where to plant the roses, which had been purchased.

It was 1922 Erna had just given birth to her son Ernst. Hilmar and his brother Hugo celebrated the event of the first male child born in the Kabaker family, and heir apparent to the business. When the baby was two months old Erna, daughter Mady, Baby Ernst, and Mathilde, the baby's nurse departed for a three weeks stay on the North Sea Island of Norderney. They traveled at first by limousine to Muenster, and then by train to Emden, where they boarded a ship to the island. The place Hilmar had rented for the family was about a five minute walk from the beach. On the next morning Erna was nursing her son, and then took the short walk together with Mady, Mathilde pushing the baby carriage to the beach. They rented a cabana (made out of basket like material). It was July, The bright sun reflecting in the wavy sea gave ample cause for relaxing and sun bathing. Mady was playing in the sand. The beach was crowded and many people walked by occasionally admiring the baby asleep in the shadow of the cabana.

In the afternoon Erna attended a beach concert, where she met a lot of people. One very respectful appearing gentleman gave her his special attention after he formally introduced himself as George von Stauss. He impressed her with being extremely knowledgeable about the many subjects of great interest to Erna. After a very lively conversation he offered to introduce Erna to horseback riding the next day, which she accepted. The next day turned out to be a most interesting one in the company of George von Stauss, and she realized that he was a man very much involved in the political and financial life of the Country.

Horseback riding was a new sport in Erna's life. She playied Tennis before and so she played a game in the afternoon with her new friend, who said good bye then, because he had to return to Berlin due to a busy schedule. He assured Erna that he would stay in touch so they could continue with their interesting conversations!

A week went by before Hilmar joined her in Norderney. They went dancing in the afternoon at a beach side café, and they had coffee, cake, and wine.

Hilmar was very proud swinging his beautiful wife to the beat of the small orchestra.. "Remember, when we visited the church in Lemgo and the pastor came to see me afterwards. I think a lot about what he said. Are we Jews closing our hearts off to this Jesus? Just think he was on this earth almost two thousand years ago. It all started in a little stable in Bethlehem. After He died on the cross, He rose again to prove that there is life after death when believing in Him." Yes," said Hilmar, "that is a very good point. I would like to talk to the Pastor myself."

Erna's greatest joy was to play the piano. She spent many mornings sitting at the grand piano in the music room of the house. Chopin was one of her favorite composers, and she was able to play some of his favorite pieces by heart. As the Christmas season approached she started practicing a number of Christmas Carols she had heard so many times played and sung by her Christian friends. Just before the holiday she asked the gardener to procure a fresh evergreen tree to fit in the dining room. Hilmar and she went shopping for ornaments, decorations, candles, and presents for family, friends and employees of the factory. Somehow they sensed that with some people it was more a custom than awareness of the deep

31

meaning upon which this celebration of Christmas was actually founded, and also the connection with the faith they were brought up to believe in!

"Let us celebrate this special time the way it should be done and invite our close neighbors and their children. Ernst was almost two and Mady almost eight years old. When all was ready and after he had lit the tree with all the wax candles Hilmar had a little bell in his hand, and he shook it to invite everybody to the celebration and receiving of gifts. There were Martha, little Erna, Marlies, Friedel and Anni, and of-course Mady and Ernst. They all joined singing Christmas carols in the music room. Then Hilmar opened the curtain and the sliding doors to the dining room, and all could see the lit Christmas tree. There were presents for all, a lot of excitement and sweets, cookies, nuts on a special plate for each of the children.

From the outset it was Erna and her husband's endeavor to participate in the community life of the town as much as possible. They not only wanted to participate but also contribute. Hilmar and his brother Hugo donated land and money to build homes for war veterans or people with a great need, a foundation consisting of a new street with homes given in the name of their late father.

The cigar factory was doing well, small manufacturing branches were established within a 20 to 50 km radius from Lemgo. Workers were hired to hand make cigars, and trustworthy employees were put in charge. Hilmar would check on it regularly. He enjoyed driving his American Pontiac and later on a light yellow Hansa Lloyd convertible with a black leather top.

As it is the custom in a lot of small German towns the "Schuetzenfest" (Festival of Marksmen) is a very happy and celebrated event; which takes place at the "Schuetzenhof" (Marksman Hall). It starts at the shooting range to establish the best marksmen and the election and crowning of the festival king. Hilmar was the captain of the second company. With his saber over his shoulder he would march in front of his company through the streets from the "Marksman Hall" to the other side of town to his house, where in the backyard a feast was prepared for the whole group of possibly sixty men. At the end of the meal all men were handed a packet of cigars, and then they all returned to the "Schuetzen

House" (Marksman Hall) for more celebrating and socializing.

Another old custom in Germany to celebrate a costume ball, called "Fasching" or "Fastnacht". It takes place before Lent (commemorating the suffering of Jesus). A big "Fastnachts" adventure had been planned by the family in a social gathering in Bielefeld. Even Erna's youngest brother, Sigfried (Siggi) was to be there, because he was employed in a department store in Bielefeld. Everybody knew Erna's costume as a Spanish dancer. After she appeared in that outfit she changed secretly again into a tree climber suit (Klettermaxe). Nobody recognized her not even her brother Siggi, who fervently courted her. She was able to change her speech to remain unknown. When it became time for everyone to take off the masks Siggi's disappointment was great, and he burst into tears.

In 1925 Erna gave birth to her second daughter Lieselotte (Lilo). She was a sweet and healthy baby. In the first year Mrs. Wiekloff, the nurse took care of her. Erna took her yearly trips to Norderney with all of her children, where her friend Georg von Stauss introduced her to many people in the arts and sports like Heinrich Schlussnus, the singer, Irene Meyer, the fencing champion and many more.

Erna visited concerts and opera performances in Hanover and Berlin.

Erna and Hilmar went hunting with some of their local friends. One of them was Ernst's elementary school teacher Hoffmann.

This was a new sport for them. Hilmar had purchased a three- barrel hunting rifle. After Erna shot a rabbit, and it was lying on the ground not quite dead she finished it off with the butt of the rifle, which broke that part of the rifle. It had to be repaired.

In 1928 a highlight in the cigar factory's history was the celebration of the 50th business anniversary with a giant party in the "Schuetzenhof" in Lemgo, with over 200 people including the many workers, friends and relatives attending. Ernst at six years old had practiced to recite a poem on this special occasion, but when he appeared on the stage he could not utter a single word. His excuse was the bright stage lights.

1929

"You better eat your supper", Mady returned: "That sausage doesn't taste good".

"It's fresh from the butcher". Insisted her mother.

With some coaxing Mady ate everything on the plate. Alas, that night Mady became violently sick. Erna called Dr. Nolting. He diagnosed food poisoning. Initially they tried to get her to empty her stomach. Unfortunately it had gone past her stomach; and the poison had entered her blood stream. Erna telephoned her father, who came from Paderborn as fast as he could. Mady was dangerously ill. Erna called Pastor Eilers. He came over to pray with mother and father. It seemed like a miracle that Mady survived and finally recovered.

1930

From the outset it was Erna's and Hilmar's endeavor to participate in the community life of the town as much as possible. They not only wanted to participate but also contribute. Hilmar and his brother donated land and money in the name of their late father to build homes for war veterans or people with a great need.

Hilmar parked the convertible on the main street in front of the apartment building, where the Goldbergs lived and worked. Then he joined Erna, Mady, Ernst, and Lilo in the dining room for one of his mother-i's meals: Chicken soup with dumplings and noodles followed by pot roast, gravy, potatoes, and vegetables. She knew how to set a tasty meal before them. As he entered the roomy apartment and passed the kitchen he could not help noticing a bearded, unkempt man in ragged clothing sitting at the kitchen table enjoying his mother in law's food. This was not the first time he saw this good hearted woman helping a beggar with a decent meal. "Hilmar, come and join us in the dining room", called Bertha. They sat around the table and talked about a lot of things. Carl Goldberg stayed longer in his medical practice, and he joined them later to enjoy the soup Bertha ladled out from a large porcelain tureen in the middle of the long extended dining room table.

Erna walked into town with Mady and Ernst to do some shopping. When they approached the Marktplatz (The square in front of the Rathaus) an unexpected large crowd carrying a red flag with a hammer and a sickle was assembled there (a meeting of the Communist Party). She got out of there as quickly as possible holding on to both children. A young fellow approached and handed her a leaflet.

Due to the weakness of the German government the country was tossed about by various political influences. When it appeared that communism could win the upper hand due to their ruthless approach to anything getting in their way of winning control several of the right wing parties decided to temporarily throw their support to the relatively small Nazi party since their method of operation, just as ruthless, could halt the threat of Communism. Never did they realize that once in a position of power they would never wane from there. Hitler cold bloodedly shot his own friend, Roehm, who was in the way of his dictatorship.

About June 1932

Ernst spent some time with his mother (Mutti) in Bad Harzburg, a spa in the Harz mountains. The great attraction was the cable car, which took you to the scenic, wooded area on top of the mountain and a likely place for refreshments.

Erna's pleasure were the tennis courts in the town's park, Ernst could recover; the balls. Then she took him to the "Kurhaus", a café with music for dancing, hot chocolate and cake. At the table next to them Ernst was intrigued by a man with an eye glass in one eye, which he never saw before. The gentleman asked his mother to dance, and became interested in her. Erna told him that she was married and also that she had a daughter. Heinz Todtmann was a journalist and an editor of a Berlin newspaper.

He later on visited the family in Lemgo, and a few years later married Mady!

Discussion between Erna and husband Hilmar: Questions Erna, :

"What is the financial situation of the firm? Hil replied:

"I think it's OK." Ern:

"What do you mean, ' It is OK?" Hil:

"Honestly I am not a trained accountant. When I look at a statement prepared by the office I am sometimes confused."

Erna:

"Why don't you let me look at it, and see if I can understand it! Isn't it rather strange that you are the head of this firm, but you are unable to determine whether the finances are in the black? Hil":

Now, please, don't make me look like a dummy when it comes to accounting," resounded Hilmar angrily. "These are not the best times as far as the economy is concerned."

THE BIG CHANGE

So it happened that the happy and trouble free years passed quickly for the Kabaker families in Lemgo, when the political arena in Germany changed over night with Hitler and his Nazi party taking control of the country in 1933.

New laws and restrictions limiting business possibilities for Jewish owned concerns, and it became difficult to operate a cigar factory successfully. Hilmar's brother Hugo decided to take his share, and to withdraw from the company.

Hilmar found it difficult running things on his own. That's when Erna decided to take over the helm. Hilmar started travelling to call on the many old customers in Germany to secure orders. Erna began to run the office, and keep tap on the day to day operations. Since the firm was now shunned by the various authorities, organizations, and banks Erna struggled for survival. The main suppliers and creditors were in Holland, who imported the select tobaccos from Dutch possessions and South America. Erna repeatedly traveled to Holland to maintain credit and keep supplies coming. She worked very hard keeping the trust of the Dutch creditors to secure further shipments, and to keep the plant going in spite of the many obstacles.

"Cronau", called the conductor, "last stop before the border."

The custom duty officers came aboard. When one of the officers spotted Erna he politely greeted her: "Good afternoon Frau Kabaker, how are you today?"

He obviously remembered her from the last time she traveled this way. They developed a friendly relationship. Erna smiled back:

"Glad to see you again, how are the wife and kids?"

"Very well, thank you!," was the reply. She remembered that this somewhat older official had been on this border duty for a long time. He had told the story of the Dutch businessman, who had a tailor in Berlin custom make a suit for him. He had only three days in Berlin, and he had it measured the first day, and there was one fitting afterwards. The tailor delivered the finished suit in a package to the train. To avoid custom duty on the new suit he went into the washroom to put it on. He took his old suit off and threw it out of the window. When he opened the package he found that the tailor forgot the pants.

Erna traveled to Amsterdam to negotiate with the Dutch suppliers. She gained their full confidence. She also visited her brother Siggi who was working for a large department store in that city. Then she returned to Lemgo and she surprised her children with some of the famous Dutch "Drooste" chocolates.

Two men and a woman were playing a card game in the lady's living room. Nalop the lawyer was with one of them, holding a big dark brown cigar between his lips pushing blue smoke into the room, and when he took the cigar in his hand to speak he exposed his tobacco stained teeth and the missing tooth on the upper jaw. The other was Dr. Hoffmann, the Syndic or representative of the employers' association of the country Lippe. He also held a cigar in his hand. Erna was sipping a cognac, and both men were drinking beer. Nalop commented: "How long can this Hitler stay up there? Something has to happen to stop this nonsense." Hoffmann shook his head: "It would be nice to know that it is just a temporary situation, and the country can be brought to normal!" Erna added: "We have to deal with the situation as it is now. I am glad we got the help of our Dutch creditors, and we can keep going even with all the hindrances."

The head office on the second floor of the M.L.Kabaker Cigar factory was engulfed in blue cigar smoke. Erna was trying out new cigars to judge their quality, which had become part of running the business. One of the production director's was sitting across from her at the opposite desk, originally Hilmar's brother's seat. The office manager brought up the latest balance sheet of the present financial situation. As Erna carefully studied the figures before her she saw that the statement showed a serious deficit. Asking further questions from the office manager she realized the gravity of the situation! She took another puff of the cigar in her hand, but suddenly she felt a pain in her chest and was overcome by a very uncomfortable and sick feeling. She slumped in her armchair and gasped for air. The men around her realized that it might be some kind of heart attack and telephoned for an ambulance.

Erna woke up in the Lemgo Hospital. She could not remember how she got there. An oxygen mask was on her face, and it was hard for her to speak. A familiar doctor leaned over her, and explained that she arrived there after she lost consciousness. She saw the relief in their eyes that she was breathing and alert. Before she temporarily fainted again she asked for Pastor Eilers, who arrived within a short time. He prayed with her. Erna asked: "Can I be baptized?" The Pastor agreed to her request. Husband Hilmar was out of town, daughter Mady was visiting friends in Berlin. A neighbor brought Ernst to the hospital, and the Pastor talked to him. After some time in the hospital Erna came home. She was very weak, and needed a lot of bed rest. It so happened that the family would have meals with her at her bedside.

Erna went through very hard times in struggling with her disenchantment with her husband. She had grown to a mature woman beyond the level of a seventeen year old girl. In addition the change of times, and the hardships due to the politics in business created a deep chasm between them!

One of Erna's admirers was Hans Hoffmann, who was present in recent months to help Erna negotiate with some of the German trade and labor organizations, and the Chamber of Commerce etc. Hans would keep her company and talk to her. He also played cards with her, which was very relaxing. He took a special interest in Erna and helped her to overcome her dilemma.

Ernst living close to his Mom could not remember when the respectful third person address was exchanged for the familiar second person (in German it is very noticeable when people are becoming more intimate with each other). Hans had taken a room in a local hotel so he would not have to commute to Detmold, where his office and home was. He also suffered from a handicap on his left leg due to polio in his youth, which kept him from driving a car. Finally Erna offered him Ernst's room in the house since Ernst slept next to her in the master bedroom. The dialog between Erna and husband Hilmar continued. Ernst remembered Hilmar saying: "I don't understand what's going on," after Erna explained their differences.

With Erna running the office and Hilmar traveling there was not much togetherness between the two of them. Their communications became limited to practical necessities like the household and business matters. Erna had always pursued her interest in the arts and helping other people. She was fostering her relationships with Georg von Stauss, singer Heinrich Schlusnus and other personalities involved in the cultural and economic life in Germany.

1934

As the cigar factory folded since Erna could no longer run it so did the marriage of Erna and Hilmar. By the beginning of 1934 divorce proceedings became unavoidable. 1934 marks the time of moving out of the grand house on Paulinenstrasse.

In Germany the beginning of the school year is right after a short Easter vacation.

Ernst started the new school year in the high school in Bielefeld, and he commuted for several months by steam train until the new family could move to that town. The new family consisted of Erna, Hans Hoffmann, Ernst and Lilo.

Mady graduated from the "Lyzeum" in Lemgo in 1932 and was now living in Berlin. She married Heinz in 1935.

Ernst's life changed drastically when he started commuting from Lemgo to Bielefeld. He had to transfer at Lage to catch the train connection to Bielefeld and there he had to get to school by streetcar. All this was very exciting. Even though the long journey to school was only temporary, it was somewhat of a novelty. Although he did not exactly understand his parents splitting up, he did realize that they were no longer compatible as man and wife. Life had become more difficult because everybody knew the Kabaker family, and being Jewish. It was easier for him to be in a new surrounding where nobody felt any prejudice against him!

———————————————

The new house was an apartment over a tavern on a main highway into the city of Bielefeld. It had a large back yard more for playing than for any particular gardening activity. The landlord was raising pigeons. They lived in a coop next to an old wall which separated the yard from an old cemetery. Ernst was able to play soccer with some of the neighborhood kids. It was more difficult for Lilo. The Hitler Youth organizations would have been the normal way of meeting new local boys and girls their age, but they had to stay distant from those affiliations.

Due to a new German law Gentiles and Jews could no longer be married in Germany. Hans and Erna flew to London (England) to be married there with some of Erna's relatives as witnesses. They started their new life in Bielefeld as husband and wife.

The Evangelical Lutheran Church, "Martini Gemeinde" was located only half a block from the new apartment. Confirmation instruction was incorporated in the school curriculum (The first class on a weekday morning). Early on Sunday morning it was Sunday school for Lilo and Ernst. The first year confirmation class attended Sunday school. Erna and Hans went to the regular worship service with the children attending also. In the process of deceiving the authorities God became the only source for help and solace. You could not miss the church bells invitation to worship. Pastor Friedrich Barnstein was no ordinary preacher. He did not pay homage to the new German regime. He was preaching the Gospel of Jesus Christ, and His love for sinful humanity. He was a follower of Dietrich Bonhoeffer's Confessional Lutheran Church: "Make Jesus the master of your life, follow Him." Romans 2/8-11 says: "But for those who are self seeking, and who reject the truth, and follow evil there will be wrath and anguish."

Lilo attended the nearby elementary school and Ernst was commuting by bicycle to the high school ("Oberschule for Jungens"). Both children adopted the name Hoffmann, and stepfather Hans became their father by name. In spring of 1935 both Ernst and Lilo were baptized in a little chapel attached to the church. Both were surprised at this occurrence since they had assumed that were baptized as babies! Hans started a new phase in his professional career, namely helping Jewish clients to maintain their businesses, or converting them into cash to take abroad. Erna was able to assist him. Most of the new clients were sent to Hans by some of her influential friends in Berlin. Her instinct in business matters turned out to be a valuable asset in her support for Hans's new calling.

The move into an apartment from a rather large house with servants brought about a huge change in life style, but it also simplified life a lot. Erna enjoyed the blessings of an ordinary housewife preparing meals, house cleaning etc. there was some regularity.

Bielefeld's interesting excursion point was the "Sparrenburg", a castle tower, a remainder of times long gone. It was built on a hill, and from its top you could see over the whole city of Bielefeld. To reach the tower you would walk through the small town of Bethel near Bielefeld. This was a settlement of homes and institutions serving handicapped people, which was founded by a Lutheran Pastor Bodelschwing, who gave it this biblical name.

Street cars made it easy to travel in the city north to south, east and west.

The apartment was on a main street on the city's south end and a streetcar would take you north to the railway station and it would take you further south to the adjacent town of Guetersloh.

Annie, a young friend from Lemgo, maintained the household when Erna accompanied Hans on business trips. The household also included Erna's parakeet, Lilo's frog, and Ernst's four goldfish and two catfish.

Annie cleaned the bread cutting machine, a round sharp disc with a hand crank. As she cleaned the crumbs from under the disc she cut her thumb. When Erna returned she tried to explain how she cut her finger and at this she cut her other thumb!

One day Erna left the kitchen window open and the blue parakeet out of his cage flew away. A few days later a green parakeet came flying in the window and he stayed.

An old man packed his backpack with strawberries, which he had raised in the garden on the side of the wall around Lemgo. He got on his bicycle, and he took the long ride to Bielefeld. He adored Erna, who had given him friendly attention during her 15 years in Lemgo. He had been somewhat of an eremitic person (a loner) living in this old wooden house along the Lemgo walls, a person avoided by society. He surprised Erna and her family: "Thanks you so much for coming all this way to see us," she said, as she was serving him food and drink to prepare him for his long ride home on his bicycle

---

In the fall of 1935 Erna and Hans decided to move to Berlin since most of the clients were there. They also found a boarding school in Bethel near Bielefeld, where Ernst could live to finish the school year and confirmation by spring of 1936.

Erna and Hans were traveling in the express train from Bielefeld to Berlin. To pass the time they were playing their favorite card game sixty six

Across from them sat an older gentleman. As he was looking at them he was amused how they entertained each other with the card game, and he addressed them introducing himself: "I am Fritz Zander." Then Erna and Hans Hoffmann responded giving their names. Just as they started to converse a man in a brown Nazi uniform (SA) opened the sliding door to their compartment. As he looked at them he mumbled an apology, and left closing the door. All three in the compartment simultaneously breathed a sigh of relief. Inadvertently a long conversation developed expressing their disenchantment with the political situation in Germany, which kept them busy till their arrival at the Zoo railroad station in Berlin. They exchanged addresses and agreed that they would stay in touch!

After getting off the train Erna and Hans took a taxi to their favorite hotel "Am Zoo" and after leaving the luggage in their room they proceeded to visit some of Hans's Jewish clients in the garment section of the city. Some of the clients were trying to sell their businesses to non Jewish prospective buyers, and to transfer their assets to foreign banks. Hans would get involved in negotiating with buyers and the governmental agency using his legal skills.

The next day Erna and Hans were searching for a suitable apartment for moving the whole family to Berlin since that was the primary hub of Hans's professional activities as a business and legal adviser They found a place to move to in the fall of 1935.

Georg Von Stauss in his top position in the "Deutsche Bank" was able to put Erna and Hans in touch with new clients.

Ever since her Illness and her baptism Erna became aware of the power of God's Holy Spirit and the influence of Jesus's teachings. Prayer became part of her life!

Ernst became accustomed to living in a boarding school in Bethel, and he commuted by bicycle to the high school, and to confirmation instructions at the church. Hans and Erna arranged a life for the family in Berlin. At Christmas Ernst traveled to Berlin to spend the holiday with the family. He enjoyed his mother's home cooking especially the traditional

Christmas goose. They attended services at a nearby church.

It had become evident that Erna was pregnant. One of the clients, Otto Jacoby insisted that Erna must be present at the negotiation in southern Germany and offered to provide a nurse if childbirth became imminent, and Erna and Hans were required to fly to Munich. However Erna was confident she would be OK. Otto Jacoby was a wealthy cigar manufacturer. He consulted Dr. Hoffmann for transferring funds into a foreign bank account, anticipating Nazi persecution of Jewish business men. He also valued Erna's judgement on anything that had to be negotiated.

In April of 1936 Ernst not only finished the school year at the Bielefeld "Oberschule for boys", but on April 5th (Palm Sunday) he was confirmed at the "Martini Kirche" in Bielefeld. He then joined his family in Berlin -Tempelhof after spending a few days with the grand parents in Paderborn, who shortly afterwards moved to be their son in Amsterdam, Holland.

On April 10th 1936 Hans-Georg was born to Erna in a Berlin clinic .

He was baptized in the Lutheran Church at "Hohenzollern Platz" in Berlin Wilmersdorf with Georg von Stauss (a member of the German Reichstag) and Otto Jacoby (a Jewish manufacturer) as witnesses.

1936 – BERLIN –

Berlin was a great contrast to living in a small or even middle size town, the hustle and bustle in the capital of the country was an entirely new experience!

There was a great excitement on the Berliner Strasse, in Berlin Tempelhof (near the airport), where the family lived now. The boxer Max Schmeling beat the American boxer Joe Louis in the USA. Hitler declared this a triumph of the white race, and he paraded the returning boxer down the Berliner Strasse past the 2nd floor apartment of the Hoffmann family, with people cheering from the sidewalk.

Both Ernst and Lilo attended Highschools (Gymnasium and Lyzeum) in Tempelhof, and when the family moved to a much larger apartment in Berlin – Wilmersdorf Ernst continued to commute to Tempelhof, but Lilo transferred to a closer location. Hans-Georg, Lilo and Ernst had their own rooms, Hans-Georg shared his room with a nurse, who cared for him in the first two years of his life. The apartment also had ample room for Hans Hoffmann's and his secretary's offices.

Travelling by bicycle from Wilmersdorf toTempelhof and to the center of Berlin and other area familiarized Ernst with the city. Using public transportation he visited the museums and exhibits downtown like the Pergamon Museum showing the excavations by Karl Schliemann.

He also ran errands for his mother and stepfather. One day when Lilo and Ernst inspected sights near the Reichskanzlei they were separated from each other by a huge crowd screaming for the "Fuehrer". Lilo inadvertently was shoved with some other young girls into the vestibule of the Kanzlei. The other girls asked to see Hitler. Luckily he was not available.

———————————————————

Father Hoffmann enjoyed to shop for delicacies at the Kempinski Delicatessen on the Kurfuersten Damm for the evening supper when he was home and not travelling to represent his clients. That was always a special event with a fresh brew siphoned from the tap of a nearby Tavern. They sat around the dining room table, held hands with a prayer, and counted their blessings. However Hans was shaking his head when it came to the political situation in Germany. Hitler is here to stay and there is no change in sight.

In 1937 Hans and Erna purchased a used Adler Diplomat automobile to help to get around to all the clients. Erna was the chauffeur. Hans's bad leg prevented him from getting a driver's license.

Erna continued to assist Hans to negotiate and analyze his professional activities with her enormous understanding and analytical mind. Whilst she at times traveled with him they employed a child nurse, Anna to take care of Hans-Georg, who was one year old.

Living in the interesting city of Berlin, revealed a cauldron where a lot of political movements had been brewing. It had a large Jewish population, and Hitler instigated Germans in general to believe that mistreating Jews would be a patriotic thing to do. Signs started to appear at restaurants, stores, and public places that Jews were not welcome.

Throughout history political leaders have been able to fire up the population in the name of patriotism to start totally unrelated movements. See also in the book of Esther (Old Testament) when Haman tried to kill the Jews in ancient Persia or the witch hunts in the 16th Century.

KRISTALL NACHT
IN 1938

Ernst went early in the morning to the bakery on the Olivaer Platz to pick up fresh rolls. A few houses down there was a Jewelry shop with the windows smashed, and people mostly men in S.A. brown uniforms looting merchandise from the display cases. Then as he returned via Kurfuerstendamm to the Saechsische Strasse he noticed similar actions at other stores which obviously had Jewish owners. This was an attempt to prevent these people from continuing to do business there, just as years before the Nazi influence stopped the Kabaker Cigar factory to function under normal circumstances!

1939

Early 1939 Mady and Husband Heinz left Germany, and found temporary stay in a camp Westerborg for Jewish refugees in Holland. From there Mady was able to travel to England at the invitation of Uncle Max Goldberg, where she gave birth to her son, John Peter on December 30th.

Her husband could not get a visa to England, and he spent World War II in that camp.

Lilo was confirmed in the Kaiser-Wilhelm Gedaechtnis Kirche at Kurfuerstendamm and Joachimsthaler Strasse

Also at the beginning of May 1939 Erna drove Ernst in the Opel Admiral from Berlin to Hamburg, where she registered him in an Interpreter School for English, Spanish, Shorthand and Typing. She also helped him to find a room in a rooming house with a nice landlady. Two weeks later Erna came back with his little brother, Hams-Georg to celebrate his 17th birthday with him. She took him on a weekend excursion to the Baltic Sea Spa Warnemuende.

Beginning of World war II

In September 1939 German troops attacked Poland. This was the news on the day Ernst completed his studies at the school. He had an invitation from his uncle Max to come to England, which could not be realized due to the outbreak of the war. He applied for a job as an apprentice in a Machine Tool Factory in Bergedorf, and he got the job, which required commuting by steam train to the suburb of Hamburg.

"Have mercy on us O Lord,
 have mercy on us,
for we have endured much contempt
we have endured much ridicule
from the proud.
much contempt from the arrogant"

(Psalm 123: 3-4)

Erna and Hans kept closely connected to Von Stauss (Who was a member of the German Reichstag). Also they still had contact with some of their Jewish friends even though in secret.

In the beginning of the war Poland was overrun by Germany from the west and by Russia from the east. It was too overwhelming for this country all at once! France and England declared war on Germany in October. It looked successful for Germany when they invaded France and drove the British across the Channel at Dunkirk.

Faith in God was the only thing that kept Erna and Hans believing that the Almighty would have the final answer!

Their friend Fritz Zander invited Hans and Erna to a secret meeting in the basement of a Church. A man spoke encouraging words:

"The Lord is my light and my salvation – whom shall I fear?

The Lord is the stronghold of my life – of whom shall I be afraid?

When evil men advance against me to devour my flesh,

When my enemies and my foes attack
me, they will stumble and fall

Though an army besiege me, my heart
will not fear.

Though war break out against me, even
then will I be confident.

Psalm 27

Erna and Hans knew what he was talking about.
It gave them hope of a solution of their present
problem but when? God's time is not measurable
by human standards. They were living out in the
open. Erna was suffering seeing the danger hanging
over their heads, hiding and making the pretense
that their lives were secure and normal. It made her
weak heart act up at times. But could anything ever
be normal when there was war and persecution by
a merciless dictator. Germans were being persuaded
that all problems could be resolved by harassing and
eventually killing all Jews and any civilized people
who objected to the dictatorship of Adolf Hitler.

Christmas 1939 the family got together and
celebrated the birth of the Savior. Ernst came from
Hamburg and they had the traditional Christmas
Goose.

A New Perspective.

Mutti, my mother and my stepfather, Vati were my best and only friends.

For along time before and during the war. I could share my frustration about our situation and they with me. I was late growing in size, and would not get enough to eat at times. My mother was saving up remainders of meals before I was able to visit them. My boss at the machine factory was generous in giving me time off between Christmas and New Year so I could be with my family in Berlin. My mother was often weak and suffering from some kind of heart problem. Her doctor and friend, Dr. Elizabeth Naegele was a frequent visitor.

Vati would usually make the breakfast, and we would all sit at Mutti's bed to eat. The main hot meal of the day would be prepared by Mutti or a cook.

On special occasions Vati went shopping at a deli for cold cuts and herring when available.

In the pre –war days Mutti chauffeured Vati in the Opel Admiral to visit various clients. When the war started the car was appropriated by the military and then they used public transportation. My mother was very outgoing and appeared energetic. She gave encouragement to other people. Even in earlier years I had trouble keeping up with her walking. She was very charitable towards less fortunate and older people. She grew up with a father, who was, as a doctor, dedicated to helping people rather than looking at their ability to pay for his services.

On our trip to Hamburg she stopped to help a down and out hitchhiker.

1941

We regularly (at least once a week) wrote to each other and sometimes telephoned. When in 1941 I was summoned to appear before the draft board I was told that as a Jew I was not eligible to serve in the German army. Within a week a policeman came to my residence and notified me that I had to wear the yellow star of David on my outer clothing. I telephoned my parents. They immediately came to Hamburg, and my stepfather tried to negotiate with the police department to no avail! They assured me not to worry, and not to wear the yellow patch. As I found out later, Vati found an employee of the "Sippen Forschungs Amt" (an Institute of the German Government to research Family origins) in Berlin to request my file from the Police department in Hamburg before it got to the Gestapo. Within a month I received a document from the draft board that my draft status was undecided, which I could produce every time there was a check up especially in trains when traveling or commuting to my work. My Stepfather laid his own life on the line to keep me from being deported to a concentration camp. My mother received a postcard from her father in a concentration camp in Theresienstadt, which was, needless to say, very neutral and did not indicate any relationship.

Also in 1941 the parents sent Lilo with Hans-Georg to Krumpendorf near Klagenfurt in Austria to stay with a family they knew with instructions that in case of anything happening in Berlin, they would have to fend for themselves. Nothing ever happened and they were OK. I was able to join them for a short vacation, which I enjoyed.

Mutti and Vati surrounded themselves with a variety of friends. There was Walter Minuth, a retired German army officer. A Navy officer and his family with a very young son, who just joined the Navy. Where did they meet those people? I don't know! There was also Dr.Naegele, Mutti's Doctor. Mutti and Vati"s social life also included persons in Government like Georg von Stauss and others. The negotiations with government agencies on behalf of his various clients in industry would bring about relations with those people. At the same time a relative of the Kabaker family, Bertha Feldheim lived at the Hoffmann apartment for a while until she found a new place of refuge.

The apartment at Saechsische Strasse 68 was also suitable for occasional parties. It had a music room with a grand piano, a "gramophone" (record player), radio, and comfortable seating arrangements. On one side it was connected by French doors to Vati's office and adjacent to that his secretary's office. The other side of the music room was also divided by French doors giving access to a large dining room. Those French doors were usually kept open. When people entered the apartment there was a reception area with a wardrobe and a washroom, which lead to a hallway with a small table and chairs and access to all the previously mentioned rooms. On the other side of the reception area was a door to the rest of the apartment. A long hallway lead to the kitchen and five bedrooms. The last of the bedrooms was the large master bedroom connected to a full bathroom, which could also be entered from the hallway. There were four floors in that building (not counting the ground floor) and two large apartments on each floor. An elevator was available. Our apartment was on the second floor. Every time I visited my own room was available (two or three times a year in the early days)

1942

1942 brought increasing air raids in the Northwest of Germany. Attacks were still rare to Berlin.

My boss Robert Blohm jr. became acquainted with my parents needing legal advice in Government matters for his plant. He traveled to Berlin on occasions, and slept in my room in my parents' apartment.

1943

Hamburg experienced an all out air raid in the summer of 1943. The attacks systematically destroyed the inner city. After two days the destruction stopped before it came to the area were I lived, when I took my bicycle and traveled through the burning city to the suburb of Bergedorf, where I worked. When I returned a few days later the house where I had lived was also destroyed, and all my belongings which I kept there. I was able to say "good bye" to my landlady, who with other homeless people was transported to a temporary shelter in another area. I found a place to live in Bergedorf first with friends, and then by subletting a garret room with another family.

The first free weekend I traveled to Berlin, where my mother helped me to purchase some needed clothing, and I also received a used suit jacket from father Hoffmann. Lo and behold on that weekend was an air attack on Berlin. A phosphorous fire bomb hit the roof of my parents house, and set it on fire. One can imagine the panic, which developed in that house. People were throwing their beddings down the staircases. My mother helped me calming down the families and to get their assistance in starting a water bucket chain. Somebody gave me a gasmask when I stood on top of the stairs in the attic squirting water with a hand pump from a bucket to keep the fire from spreading until hours later the fire department extinguished it completely. My mother was the last person in the bucket chain, who handed me the full buckets of water. It was also helpful that the attic was empty and the woodwork had been covered with fire resistant tar, which dripped on the back of the suit jacket, I wore and had just received from my stepfather, I continued to wear it.

Air attacks on Berlin intensified, and when I could not reach my family in Berlin after heavy bombing on November 25 I got permission from my boss to travel to Berlin on local, slow moving trains. It took at least 4 to 5 hours instead of the 2 hours on the express train in normal times. When I finally arrived at the Charlottenburg railroad station, I had to walk the remaining 4 miles until I finally stood in front of the remaining front wall, which used to be my parents house. At that point I was overcome by the deep shock, thinking that everybody was dead! I broke into tears.

However my great sorrow was replaced by great joy when suddenly my parents appeared alive and well. Mutti had saved some belongings from the apartment, and they had a place in the basement of the "Rassen

Politisches Amt" (Race Political Office of the Government) almost next door to the destroyed residence, where they had stored their saved belongings. That day and few days afterwards I stayed with Mutti and Vati at the luxurious villa of the Zander family in Berlin Dahlem. Of course in the nights were more air attacks and we would move to the basement of the villa. I remember using the huge bathroom with the sunken bath all in Italian marble. There was only cold water as existed everywhere. The day after I arrived I was able to recover a very large wooden box from our basement section of the destroyed house, which contained my sister Mady's household articles, which she left behind before leaving Germany. These were the only things like knives, forks, table cloth etc., which they could use when establishing a household in a sublet apartment later on. After few days in Berlin I became very ill, and since I became too ill to go to the basement at the Zander home my mother took me back to the basement of the "Rassen Politisches Amt". She summoned a local doctor, but he was unable to diagnose my problem. She knew of a Jewish doctor (Dr. Segal), who determined that I had some type of jaundice and needed to be in a hospital. My mother immediately had me transported to the nearby Catholic St.Getrauden Hospital, where I spend over a month past Christmas recovering. The nuns were very nice and caring. The air raids continued and all the patients were brought into the basement when the sirens sounded the alarm. I remember one elderly room mate did not make it back upstairs, because he passed away during a raid. My mother came to see me regularly. When I finally recovered enough to leave the hospital I was very weak. Mutti put me on a train to Mohrungen in East Prussia,; Where Lilo and Hans-Georg were staying at the time. I cannot remember how long I stayed in Mohrungen. Mutti came and checked up on her children and then I returned with her to Berlin and then to Hamburg on my own.

1944

The Hoffmann's found another place to live, subletting a furnished apartment near their old address. There even was a grand piano, which meant a lot to my mother. Playing the piano was a wonderful outlet for her to relax. Mutti had continuous health problems, which made her spend more time in bed. It did not help when the man from the "Sippen Forschungs Amt" visited them with the results of his research into the Jewish descent of the family. He demanded money to keep quiet about it. Luckily Mutti and Vati had enough to keep him satisfied! Then there was the sudden death of their friend, Georg von Stauss due to some lung complication. He was 65. He would have been the last resort, when danger from the authorities would occur.

Germans in general were facing hardships. Shortage of food etc. daily air raids, losing loved ones in the attacks and at the fronts.

Vati continued to travel to Munich, Magdeburg, and other places to negotiate for clients etc. Mutti and Vati traveled to Baden-Baden to recover from some of the strain of their lives. When I think of it to-day I am amazed how they managed? Vati overcome the pain in his bad left leg. There always was the fear of discovery, but help was just a prayer away! Letters received in the beginning of the year described continued air attacks, which destroyed a substantial part of the houses and buildings around them. My parents were all worn out because of the lack of sleep. Vati's letter of February 2nd and Mutti's letter of February 3rd told me of the unbelievable destruction, which took place around them in the last few days. The "Rassen Amt" was finally destroyed and they were able to save their last belongings and took them to the basement of their newfound residence at Emserstrasse 19/20. Vati's office in that house had been finished by a bomb explosion.

It was always difficult for us children to fully comprehend the enormous worries and difficulties our mother and father had to overcome in dealing with the many problems, which occurred in those days.

Their deep concern was to keep us all alive through these years. Reading the many reports made it quite clear that the Allies were advancing, but there was simply no telling when peace would come. Mutti found it especially hard to be so long away from her youngest son, Hanne (Hans-Georg). In her letter of February 12th she wrote to me:

"Lilo will bring Hanne to us and then we'll go to Baden-Baden. How glad I am to have the boy with me again. Just think how bad it would have been for you at his age to be away from me so long."

But I know that it was her deep seated Christian faith and trust in God, who would make all things work for good for those, who love Him (Rom. 8/28} This was something Mutti passed on to all of us, and she stayed close to all by her letters, when she could not be near us. The cheerful and upbeat letters from my parents kept me, and probably Lilo and Hanne patient and understanding. They spent about three months in Baden-Baden. Hanne stayed with them, Lilo went back to Mohrungen until her job ended there about two months later. Vati traveled to different business appointments in Berlin, Munich, and Magdeburg, and he would intermittently return to Baden-Baden. Lilo found employment in a children's home in Baden-Baden and Hanne was able to stay with her.

Our parents finally decided to return to Berlin permanently at the end of May. However, Mutti became seriously ill with some kind of thyroid problem, and they had to find a specialist to help her. She was able to return to Berlin after the sixth of June (last letter from Mutti in Baden-Baden). I was able to visit Berlin about the middle of June to recharge my Batteries or to get revitalized and strengthened physically and spiritually. They always had some extra food for my stomach and my soul. It was probably just a weekend. I hated to leave, but I returned in good spirits. According to the letters from Berlin, Mutti went to Baden-Baden to pick up Lilo and Hanne and bring them to Berlin. I visited Berlin at the end of August and then again in November likely on the weekends. I also spent some time with them at Christmas with our fervent hope for peace! Lilo and Hanne spent a lot of time with friends in Ferch, a place outside of Berlin, just to keep them away from the constant very destructive air attacks.

1945

In the beginning of February 1945 I received an order from some government authority to report to a work camp in Hamburg for rubble clean-up. I conferred with my parents on a weekend, and I did not know that this would be the last time I saw my mother. We felt certain that the end of the war was close, and my mother assured me that they (the family) would be with friends in the country, when the Allies would be advancing on Berlin! I informed my boss, Mr. Blohm of my impending departure to a work camp, and he arranged for an interview with a Gestapo agent in Hamburg. For some reason in answer to my prayers he believed my story, and let me continue with my work at the factory.

In her last letter of February 21st my mother wrote:

"With all the discomfort of the present critical and uncertain situation and future, all things will work for good, and I am certain and believe in a good ending. We are all quite well and we think of you often. I am particularly worried about your wellbeing."

The last letter from Berlin before the end of the war was written by Vati, who had been traveling and was in bed recovering from the strain. Amongst other things he wrote:

"Our dear God protected Mutti, Lilo and Hanne, when last Tuesday. March 20th not fewer than 29 bombs came down near Emserstrasse, one of them, a land mine on Emserstrasse 17, destroyed all windows, window frames and curtains in our house."

Mutti wrote a greeting at the bottom of this letter.

THE END OF
WORLDWAR II

On April 30th 1945 Berlin capitulated to the Russians, and the British Army entered Bergedorf, I was aware of their presence at my friends, the Dalldorf's house, which was across the street from the police station and the town hall. I was very happy and grateful, it felt like a heavy burden fell off my shoulders.

The British occupation forces in the area came from Newfoundland, and since all work at Blohm had stopped, I found temporary employment as an interpreter. About five months passed, and I received no word from my parents from Berlin or wherever they had been at the end of the war. There was no official way of communication like writing letters, telephoning or whatever, and the only thing for me was to travel to the Eastern Zone of Germany and to Berlin.

On a brisk fall night in October I and other travelers climbed on an open freight train car, partially loaded with coal at the main Hamburg rail road station destined for Helmstedt, the town before the official east-west border. By daybreak I and a great number of border crossing people were met by a Russian guard, who raising his rifle ordered us to stop. I and a couple of fellows hid in the bushes whilst the great numbers of border crossers were herded by the Russian guard to a central location. We were able to board a local train destined for Berlin. I finally made it to Wilmersdorf, Emserstrasse 19/20, my parents last known address.

My Stepfather, Lilo, and Hans-Georg were alive, but my mother was missing. She was last seen on April 25 talking to a couple of SS soldiers trying to persuade them to move their ammunition and gasoline trucks, which were parked in front of the house. I cannot describe how I felt at this very devastating news, but at least I can try. I felt that a major part of my world had suddenly been ripped away from me. I fought the idea that my mother was really not there any more. I followed all possible clues and one of the next steps was to talk to the Sisters and nurses at the nearby St. Gertrauden Hospital. I found out that a Mrs. Hoffmann with her legs blown off by a bomb was brought in on the 25th of April, died there on April 27th and was buried in a mass grave in the courtyard of the hospital. The Sisters had tagged all jewelry of their dead patients for future identification, because so many people died at that time. Unfortunately, the incoming Russian soldiers took all the valuables. I thought of the golden cross always hanging on Mutti's neck on a golden chain, her silent witness to her Christian faith. No sacrifice was ever too big to serve her family, even her life. Her love and resourcefulness helped us all to survive the years, when we were living on the edge!

"Greater love has no one than this, that he
lay down his life for his friends."

(John 15:13)

I know Mutti saw the importance of persuading the soldiers to move their vehicles, loaded with gasoline and explosives, away from the apartment building to preserve the living quarters of her family, and she ignored the danger she was in. Her passing created a great void in the lives of her children especially in the development of her nine year old son, Hans-Georg. Even her husband Hans changed into a different person without her influence on his life!

We thank God for our mother. She left an indelibly bright mark on all of her children, and we will cherish her memory until the end of our days.

EPITAPH

This was written since there is no grave and headstone with Erna's name on it. The remains of the mass grave at the St. Gertrauden Hospital in Berlin-Wilmersdorf were individually transferred to the Wilmersdorf Cemetery. They were marked as persons unknown, who died during the last days of World War two. One of them is Erna's Grave.

Epilogue

Part of this story is a figment of my imagination, how I think it could have happened!

How did my mother, who was raised in a Jewish World develop such a keen interest in Christianity? I have tried to visualize her history, her youth, her life, how she met her first husband, and some other incidents without knowing whether everything happened exactly as I described it. All I know for sure that she genuinely accepted Jesus Christ as her personal Savior before Hitler's power became so overwhelming in persecuting Jews.

Her genuine and deep seated faith should be a guiding beacon for my extended family for generations to come! Even her first husband asked to be baptized just hours before he left Germany to escape to Sweden!